D1595627

UGLY DUCKLING PRESSE

gowanus atropolis

JULIAN T. BROLASKI

gowanus atropolis
© Julian T. Brolaski, 2011, 2020

ISBN 978-1-933254-81-4

First Edition, 2011
Second Printing, 2020
Printed in the USA

Ugly Duckling Presse
The Old American Can Factory
232 Third Street #E-303
Brooklyn, NY 11215
uglyducklingpresse.org

Distributed in the USA by Small Press Distribution
Distributed in the UK by Inpress Books
Distributed in Canada by Coach House Books via Publishers Group Canada

This book was made possible in part by public funds from the New York City
Department of Cultural Affairs in partnership with the City Council.

To Mary Begley

contents

elegy

gowanus

manahatta

pseudarchipelago

gowanus atropolis

elegy

timor yorkis

gardens under lock and key
timor yorkis conturbabat me

thou angler in a lake of darkness
—flesh and fell—
bemonsterrd lordily

and wen I am attired, thus arrayd
I sing for pretty things—tutivillus
rimmed by concrete blast walls
and concertina wire

once they are not pre-disassposessed
—n CREEP inna dark corner
tippling amoebic rockets
in the green zone

& horns attonce
what purpose do they serve
but atop a moose
to think that I *suffer for nature*
—indecorously the human abode its

fingernail portrait
a sober business in york
flawd tearducts
and fake virginity

babyperson

I've a thing for entitled urchins.

—Kate Colby, *Unbecoming Behavior*

the offal of gold
—perpetuity anon
                —embraced in parts
tech support in tatters

dont want the ppl who
dont want you
the actual potato
who on and off are not even listening
tied on
in 'peace'
succumbing to subpar meat

effit on the avnue
to 'keep it lo'
xe calls xemself a 'singersongwriter'

allalong awwful // by shades
        mercy
as uttered by orbison
cherry cola to rhyme w/ l-l-l-lola
melodious offal, the kind of content you flip thru backward
        one harumphs
                uneasily along

who to hold doors for
who to allow to hold
        doors for

the way to be
a fool with a tool
who admit to not even listening
to thir own babyperson

going around adding –ess to nouns
lion-*ess*
poet-*ess*

thats such a load
so that the daffydill yawns back
the one who taught me greek is dead
you want to put them in your lap

if s/one is mocking let it be tender

for T. Peterson

so what if the magistrate calls you dude
for all the petrogaff in helsinki
what is the idles, the ides to you
the hottest month on record

if s/o is making a mockery
& yew liable to get thwarted
one needs a quiet room
who hands out thir fucking pronoun paradigm at parties??!!

if s/o is mocking
let thir hart be tender
harted. if one can be
not-deformed.

not/quite (cows in texas)

whats lost in the pasteurization
whats left hanging by its
neck in the pasture
whats left but to censure
whos left in the pasture
the cow ringing its neck the cow
ringing its hands
the air wincing w/
newest snow, not quite
snow
when the mixture has reduced
snu in hand
when the pasture
confounds the sailor
when hemoglobin hits the racks
and the cow bleeds
and the cow
not quite dead in the machine
but the cow is—and I
o cow   I
I vow
I vow to see cow as cow
in amarillo
n/thing but beef and god

buried at sinrise

optimouse
        many beasts
                forlorn around the altar
many boast   belief
        madhatter   keep

how rhodes is   sst—
          —cavalier—
many-hearted disgrace   so that
        many ran whan they were like to balk

          —beasts among—
            eat and drink heartily

     friends furred and unfurrd
     my present page   in l-l-livery

liminal   ack   posserity

      divest by number
      and no sunner

the borrower is buried at sinrise
     who bravd the neck
          —beastly—

there is a soul I

there is a soul I'd like to meet
a part or glance I'd bury
in the earth discreetly

queynte and buttoned
say yr long and a-
long say cdju?

awash in petrodollars
over the lee
end of the lake

of all the wounds, this one   this one

storial waltz
wastrel asteroid
I tied one on in arcadia tonight
one flew off the handle at the vista
& went in brave like costa brava

well one goes merrily along
who never bit thir nails
over aristotle

honduray, along the way
you'll never turn your back on me
when I play the drums

alphalegions to the max
an actual arctic wind
an arctic wind in actual

4 packs of honey down the throte
4 packs of honey down the maw
4 packs of honey down the gullet
4 packs, grade A, savannah georgia

last swan of avon

socalled swan of avon
n/t but a beaurocrat
buggering the buttercups
goy from the waist up

now soldiers're the ones making offers
and fucking caravaggio posters
maybe the artist had bothered about melancholia

suddenly xe finds xemself walking down
some dark corridor

california was truly the promised land
for a minute there
video marlboro
to show us

shoppingcart in dingy water
and then turn melancholical

sign reads no squatting
switchd on the cathode ray
at yr coronation

the bomb droppd w/ regular monotony
leaving us wanting

        a to zed
dampened a grid

satyrical deliria
pan's baallet
in a black tutu

who have the inclination
but even whose   necromancer—
firelit but dred—
—commandeering meadows—
protests were pathetic

bridge to nowherr

a lack of willingness, if you will
makes es wooing parlous
john henry or john kerry
a mystical wonderhaus

of wonderments in maine
who demand the desegregation of
washrooms, who swindle a soup
xir showers and xir shammies
one star in thir square of skye

the warrish norm wit bloodyed head
armadillo holding a turtle—
—the eye and its waterspout—
cleopatra's asp, or wotever
hecuba's neckjob

s/thing too luxuriant
w/ a blade
and s/t too capitulative
with a moose

Θanatos yo

adversaries of use
not onlye thot on thir constituents
whan who
who do not agree as to yoots
the pickling one has nat done
Θanatos, top oxling
wot offers thirself
when even achilles
looks on them lustily

when one is trampled by the hounds
of a clumsy lorry

one submits they are of lesser mind
than this companye
but one has an other crafte
far better to creep in the high grass
of hysterical illnessess

that mountebanke
causeth the invention to become tangible
who hurle brodesydis at eche other
break you off a
goodly hunk—
luck is just
a residue of the brine

blackwater stole my pronoun

abysse in fr. refers to the sea specifically
as opposed to a crevasse on land
how we say the grand canyon
or credit ratings are abysmal

one can be in a abîme, complete ruin
as jwlhyfer observd
once you start fucking in the bed
the relationship's over

blackwater stole my pronoun
as february unclenches its fist
like hitler using 卍
like martial's plagiarius

the pit of tutivillus

todo el tiempo quelque new atrocity
met w/ flies
the seer wit understanding
almost undercut hir prophecy

my muzzle will be made of moss
in the whinter
you think it's *music* but it's like lilies when they fester
all ovular moonlight tusking the apparatus

when I say lily I do mean the same
swete my sweteing
each arm asway on tender footing
who alone is burning plastics

california as arcadia

the bees are all dying my darling
dying, the bees are and I am
and you, and me, and em—
why die? why bees die?

the bees are all dying my darling
dying, the breezes yarr and lea
in a restive sunni town
east of the euphrates

astonishd fish

(after Maria Esther Maciel's 'Peixes perlexos')

The fish love to be around those rigs!
xxxx–John McCain (17 September 2008)

the eyewall favorable for
ikonicity   an
ambivalence au bibliothèque
how eche rig shattrs
the hrt & the gut & the spleen
of fanny-freddy infamy

the fish begin to speak queerly
something that never will happen before
alexander the great
my contemporary
girding the neck
au quelque crossroads
wot disgorges
the libertine's lap
n the ganymede's hole

mariesther asks *why were the fish not given any tediousness*
indemnification and not being held
harmless
then what the heck ys love
my brinkly protocol?

gowanus

where the gowanus splits in twain

for dear Dana (w/ thanks to Alice Notley)

we've all crossed thresholds we dont brag about
iphegenia oxling
when arbolaf dies
one is hailed to arden
as one goes hitherto
asphyxiating along the gowanus
in spite of that rat light
in the gutted yardland
or where jackadaws coo
in concrete galoshes

here where the canal splits in twain
where no bivalves gurgle at our kushing
—crawfish p.o.v.—parted hair—
a candidate for the cabinet
sunken bicyclette
an ackshul xerox of a great grandparent
sure I remember the gasgauge
but it had all the appearance of gog

fin city

for Sludgie

fools press
down so hard
in spring, sunshine redress

sepulchre wot leaves
sludgie
marinetied

these itinerant times
one's yukked getting
toxicity

the whale what ate it
in the gowanus
like to be

shapely
sucking scum in its teeth
picking out bottletops

gowanus apocalypse

bees at toledo
gog and magog
satellite—farce
spycams ablog
as they drip w/ pearls
and molt

landlord   peraventure
infinite   di—a'ready—
harry   harry
ope   myopia
ersatz   rigeur

> gays throw shade on the
> heart to cover
> goosefoot   magoo
> lineal   delionation
> fugg. forlorn.

gag & how could I
surfing wit

4 score diadems, falcon
four-and-twenty elders

ersatz chartreuse   diamond in whore-diadem
crinoline   cantelope   sitting on the waters
        ipode cantilever   curls bewray
pretty earlobe disgrace—federico—

the buffalo I foment about, wildly
the torture taste of pâté
shard parade
along the gowanus

calliope anon   areft
misanthrop   nebuchadnezzar dreams on
margaritas-to-go   blind—behead—the messenger
brangelinə   boxoffice
minnie pearl   autoharp avec

how a dog plays tennis
how a gog, magog
if xe has nails
to standit
industrial pawwipe

sludgie, anon!

how a dog goes
we go thru anon

antique roses and lambsquarters
the gowanus'
fecal matter percentage
proteus wo
kristelnacht gauntlet
of liquorsoaked amulet-tennis

mesoteric
acrostic dawn

what we hang on anon, 311
we crouch in tha kitchen, adept
as silverfish

sludgie being
erato anon—snu backhand
how a dog—southie crossd—
vesuvius eros—greasepaw—
    —ass singed & boiled—

serve—snarlemane
prim raintalassa
the dolla one dolla
summer is afterr

zinc, hazard of
chicken heralded—purple sea—hold my calls

acchh agog—eruvia
                flavia   pigsweed—goosefoot among

proteus wd if eratus—
—peeled of hir shortstockings
d'artagne   rust
thistleloo

h-m   madonna
humidlockd   magda-in-green
complete   like federico
w/ parrot   the courtier
fingering   thir tassle

cryptoquotation agnaw
honeybees gurgling
in ersatz anglonorman
bovary cum ratatouille
pitbull T-O-G

all ridded of giggling
anthropormorphia aghast
DL in the bowries
googling tee hee

wicked hee
to bury our hart at
our hart was in our knee

to be kush is not to be chronic

to be kush is not to be chronic
I'd lay all my ganger upon it

that twerps are <u>most</u> <u>like</u>
to be ethical creatures

it only leaked inordinantly
my time stricture had a habit

wanton until noon
wel cd they speke englysshe

polymorphously, it's the juice
n I stand by my ambivalent sidekick

beat up for being the wrong kinda pretty
outlander skeeters suck after

princes reginae

piscium et summa genus haesit ulmo / nota quae sedes fuerat
columbis / et superiecto pavidae natarunt / aequore dammae.
(fish caught in the elmtops / which once were the
dwelling of doves / and frightened deer / swim in
the seas)
            —Horace, Ode 1.2.9-12
xxxx

      wronk of airs   tomtomfoolery becuz
diss fortune

cold cold ♥
if I had yr
        apoplexy ashes
           dissassemblé

what'err I had
compromised my ease

        damesirs of fishairs
about to pinpoint treason
zun'zunism   arust

        limbed elms
        colluding w/ doves
        what folly else
           ich hadde

limbd—sparrow—was
        juvenile hunchback
        hirondelle minke
        petite baleen
        thrashing at the mouth of the gowanus

low   a lowing

              all'arche
a queen's a sparrow's hairline
           thir chartreuse archery gloves

             elizabethe
                  myn eye

twill never hurt   alack   areft
regina prince
          locks beset
          candle agrove
                a buck in a corridor

now I'm yr dad

with xir mind on xir money and xir money on xir mind.
xxxx–PFJ cum Snoop Dogg

either doggeard to be comic
or spaciously an ape attracted to beauty
hurld in the hadean eye
for a cue to being modern
bathing in like total myopia
the smaller eastern atlantic shells
and the narrow alpine strawberries
one draws forth from the banks
irrevocably one's hauteurs

murder on the gowanus

swell me a bowl
with lusty oil
brightest under bis
geynest under gore

ecce who com
inna persian vestment
un monodatal voll
marines cd not hoist thee

whose eyes go seaward   noreaster reeling
thrashing at the mouth of the gowanus
mischance upbrimmd

sludgie helas, aloft
sometimes honeysuckle can smell like MURTHER

yr shining form to oil hath returned
yr helmet now shall make a hive for bees

it was no dream   I lay broad waking
oil blossomd green, incarnadine

s/thing keeps
on testing me for tb

is politer not to talk about
beastly p.o.v.

ludic
like a succubus vomiting ivy
lordly subtler
grotesquerie

you can bet it smelled like murther
creped and crinolinnd along the noggin
w/ a victorian western pin

till I may see a plumper sludgie swim
everlike rotund
buddha—smack aghast
everlike leo and thir friends
marching in lockstep
to the sunlit uplands

dead end graffitos & gingkos on the gowanus

truck and its substance
gowaANas
is for
BrokenhHeARTs

A [narchist]rch
Deluxxe

deth
rult
mishət
nishət

gowanuscatz
blu sky
calico bitches
ERF

gowanus atropolis

the bees are up to their knees
in a noxious nectar

cantilever / squad in legion
a hero   a snifter
                        covetous chartreuse
grist for whales
fair harlot by the heels of thir gullet

filibuster cointreau
an eve-enning emma
marquise-covered leather
escargot cab
and ivan, ivan the terrible

even plagues cast waves
        locusts in hyena-guise
ephemeral as whaleroad
a halloo as wd like to greet granada
        a test of quills
to which the beast took no bolder part
irie member of blunt fame

tho egg I had proven
                meander the bandit
juan dos pistolas
in crinoline fashion

evangeline the lesser you
        harmonious and ungrateful tablet!

                    astoria the nerve
                    gimlet whalesong
sheetmate the noive
             nimbed saints on spiral waves
esperelion the dandy fashioning
             apocalypse tables—

malenervée   the noive
elemental   handservant
moralistic   vulgar piehole
piqued   primerole
prim   confessional
eureka   eurydice

adverse yaw

what dairy melts most neatly and most easily
a product or a person
aзens / avec kynde
for or against nature
to act in opposition to one's genitals

turn your cock inside out and get a cunt like a prius
vs. take some cuntflesh and get a cock like the wright flyer I
@ kitty hawk
with adverse yaw
wingwarped
circumnavigated
how to fashion
a canard

dont you need a machine or a bedazzler
awaiting blooddrawing at the queer center

the pythia poised over greekish fumes
martini slick as the gowanus with oil

with what one engenders one
is
adore
adorabile

netherlandish grotesques
blue lobster and decrepit seathings

the secrets of dyestuffs
in the popish cape
the angel rubbing itself onna nob

elegy for kari edwards

for memorial at Zinc Bar, 23 June 2007, NYC

I am your sugarplum fairy commodore in chief.
xxxx–kari edwards

conturbabimus illa.
(*vivamus, mea Lesbia, atque amemus* [let us live,
my Lesbia, and let us love])
xxxx–Catullus V.11

damesirs of fishairs
princes reginae
I dont need this botheration
guilded toe in a gendered pension
embedded narcissism
skirts can or could be worn w/

intentional disgrace
getting oh-aff
I sleep where I sit
gog and magog
ope myopia

sweetness and delight do
it for sidney, as starlover did rue
on star, thir mistress cloying
the lack, with thir poesis toying

twill never hurt
regina prince
alack, areft
locks beset
candle agrove
a buck in a corrider

as like with likeness grace the tongue
and sweets with sweets cloy them among

conturbabimus illa
let us confound them

beasts implored and character impaled
agathas breast in a 14th century pincer anon
7 heads w/ 7 comings on
horns on their horns
wings at their feet and at their wings

well you have three seconds to live
bespeckled apprentice
freckled daylilly
a penny uneasily
pleaded myrtle

iron bootblackening
at the speed
we levatate con
there is no missus
I am among

limbed elms
colluding with doves

nor tide nor tail
angels w/ svelte angles

the rub and tug goils
languid as jersey
too early for supper

etc was their pimp
and whatever their sucker
shitslinger
master cleanser

w/ corporate coffee
and torture pâté

my present page
in l-l-livery

old glut
of a beast's spleen
the glory over
lordling socked ajaw

nassau ablog
by fairly a sweepmate a swoopster
bedevilled in gullet
swashbuckld by proxy

homosexuality eh?
red river andaloos
funny albeit friday
all the dork-rock

gender suggests
we levitate avec
held captive
patrón, bothermonger

ah myrtle
why sie is taken
my mind
impertinent parasol

glossy wit promise of salt
caint leave thir cellphone alone
ipode eterna
satellite viscera

muscadetted papillon (that one)

strident
17 stallions
with horns on their heads
and horns coming out of the horns

a papillon
that one

a buck in a corridor
conturbabimus illa
let us confound them

all ridded of giggling
anthropomorphia aghast
DL in the bowries
the tee hee ambigenuity
of amputee-wannabees

googling tee hee
silly faggot
dicks are for chicks
dicks are for chicks

wicked hee
to bury my heart at
my heart was in my knee

manahatta

freedom isnt free

wimp become hunk
omfg in a pneumatic tube
most aggressive city
m-m-m-my core-english

albeit of earth
mor like a dripping
anchor o'er the oarrod

this my monthly milk threshold
contempt and seasonal
like dora in hir wanted milieu
to each thir blasphemy,
thir gormless weblog, thir merry-goe-sorrow

I have to become more like my doppelganger
filled up with philosophy
who says of bananas
the bruisd part's the sweetest

little eephin annie

a web of antonyms pervades the scenery
we lash the sea like xerxes

babybug, babybug
little eephin annie

a duplicate name
exists on this network

translocating the thorax
in the hinter of manahatta

the wren went scooting along—
that too will join the archive

myths of manahatta

Sarah Bernhardt is spending her Summer vacation on
the coast of Brittany, where her principal diversion
consists in shrimping and rambling among the rocks.
xxxx–*NY Times*, 'The Indians of New York City,'
xxxx 12 September 1897

from the woodlands of new york
lenape nation
sovereign L-train

the weckquaesgeeks
& reckgawawancs
& melville's 'manhattoes'
mahicans   mohegans
unami   munsee delawares
lenni lenape
oneida   cayuga
onandaga seneca
mohawk

usually just 'indians'
'basically algonquins'
'were' residents

the kapsee group of canarsie
said to have sold manahatta
for '60 guilders
worth of trinkets'
for which the deed was never found

& the dutch west india co.
'for goods worth $24'
promptly applied
the paleface theory of ownership

apoplectic l-l-livery
scourge of mannahatta
vanishing thereto

'for 60 guilders worth
of trinkets'

dont we all literally
live in huts

gotham in arrears

since one immured is not forgot
I let a pansy wilt for rot

and vowed the banker's misunderstood
what crowned the leafy brays of cottonwood
let all the trim gone daisies
be forgot. let bloodbaths
fill the dailies

all incognitos arrayd
we swim thru the hudson only
to find the golden egg

variations
on the acanthus, bear's breech
a boar in the group. old spies
have a habit of blunt speaking

moore said of
their pub in the glen

taliban normally carry out fresh
attacks w/ the thaw

there will be
increased snow
over the lee
end of the lake

opticianry in yorkville

like the ramble
carl schurz park's

famed for
buggery

trimmed by giuliani
not not getting some

the barber tells me
I dabble in opticianry

selly maillarde
blindies near the board

to the putch
hir shutterybuggery

millefeuille herm
& goat at the ends of mannahatta

pseudepigraphia
attributed to plutarch

who believes
in parallel lives

autobulus and ammonius
pithy delphic

all spyes for the metropolis
its edge

androgundd tompeepery
    —suuu'eh! greekish-roman

had not the thot

waited for some moments t'arrive
whan one has leve to be
quiet to be whol

the carapace one comes
nat acrosse
holey moley to the muggers who
surrounded one in the murk

I look uphudson
downriver
anchorage
ys in alaska

I have not tried to make my handwriting any way
I have not even succeeded in clearing
the drugs from my body

the thot, the dirge in question
freedom will be larger
than its twin

one had not the thot
twas a symbology
erected in (my) brayne

one had not the pathos
n/t dangled from
not downy fur
nor nor

one had not the thot
ther was no umbrage
not not not a person
merely an achorage t'uphold

imagine having to strap down
disloyal protruberances
forneo est no thing
I fancied I cd smell the bacon from there
or I cd smell bacon but it was not the same bacon

damesirs of fishairs

that the camera is—most at odds—
        meme I   unmerriwether
              the dog w/ just a feather
              for its kerchief
misserrs upon the poetesses
      in feverish redresses (~~only just~~ spared
one has (in service) tybil serviced
            in pretty pennyeyes

        un-dewar the goer
           make of xem a fishtale
                (most ravenous)
my delibel ynke
        wot rougher / humorless
        has ravvened
    the stench of this city   its verticality

fools act so hard

what, for a fool to act so hard
saying no *they* will go get the wine
leaving notes around like
let cash be earned while you're sleeping or cruising

you can do better
I began to gather all my hands and malodorous shoes together
petrified mulberry, crocus in clay

what makes hard fools to be wearing such motley scrappery?
we all decant our prophecy in ratjars
cowering behind the tain

portrait of brittany at the vma awards
                            —long bleak queer derailment—
as one who gets high on frottage

apex
            telemundo
the word as it was writted on waking—
                            lillotry

betides the rhymes on the train are fake
continually going toward woodlawn and never arriving
a hilite in the dramedy
we rapture under waves of lilletry, snap

nurse on the defense
            yr ill toil
as one who on waking revelld

how the siberian tiger transgressed its compound
people call here wanting monty

a personnage or object inches toward an other
blood, vomit, the sound of someone having a cow
sudoku lost in the smell of fish

retrograde canon

beckett's breaking ball
leaves audibly falling
—blake with knees buckling—

mowers w/ bipolar attitude
keeping the infield sexy

what do we know about putin's soul
heavy expletive in circles
the gospell of the gipper
musharraf visibly sweating

what tune nero fiddled
when rome was burning
m-moderato cantabile
drunk onna glass of buttermilk

uncelestial haste
confused at the plate
firecrackers lo to the ground
what-cheer

tankard of ocean
enhutched
in manahatta

all talent is liquid trouble
we confide against

the wildering of manahatta

manhattan was a vast forest
of oak maple chestnut and pine
very well
abounding in berries

river that flows both ways
innumerable porpoises
sweet air flooded
w/ whippoorwills

beauteous algonquinesque
painfullest of mayberries
homily reforested   rodefuckd
ottering the mob

the myth of the subway

funnyface barbers, us
wimp become hunk
omi the tanline
turtle inna pneumatic tube
engorging softserve snowlilies
coney island bound q train
rats rush the copper platform

efficiency module in liberty city
cop syndicate w/ hunk output
I'm paranoid, but not paranoid enough
eyes in the pigeons, eyes in the trees

cameras surround the mayoral compound
we stuff our face w/ watercress
exclusive to our paranoia

fed up w/ our own cappadry
extinctifying the honeycomb
w/ crapshoot cavalry
bare minimum LED

springhood and heir irwin

springhood warbles thrice and when it coos
too whoo, ta'woo
too whoo tuuu hhwweeuuuwww eeeerrwing
tuh'woo irrwin!

cracked guitar
w/ its desiccated sponge
the several gelid squirrells
acrobattic

picnickedlike eat
willownut meat
and nekkid songbirds
wrestle the outcome

tawoo hoo, earwig! and woo, irwin!
here come th'enamorous springhood
in person, herr errwhig themself
in person, heir irwin!

eidolon you dote on

for Etg

certifiably dose
a bugger in t—aviator guise—
tho the foodstuffs be lowly
and rank in variety cumberly

more of the same
long rat—
shepherd—
pile of cats

weasle thru the narrows
the stench of tuscany

fixicity

                a tug of one's

blueberrian avaunt

             hamardian—thugboat

apocalypse avowd to the threshold of credulity
          promisd a pillow during one's flight
        satan or xemu

that apparent

          anxiety of perversion

  person inna hazmat suit, far from home
        frost heaves in the hinter
      eidolon you dote on

jamjar in harlem

stefani, one is isolate even unto company
        reiphigenated among the bedbugs
and motley, luci@ strawberry

              from one nomenclature to another
              that shit was alcæic

              that kathy really is chatty

              ope myopia
              ersatz chaleur

              what spanish harlem attenuated
              biterminous council

              salad w/ beluga oil
              whale in one's jamjar

one gets wrestled into seeming curfew
n cough behind crackd storm windows

getting ready to be serious w/ lambsteak
              xe dismantleates the jamjar

abreast the stoic ends of manahatta

pill what assoils guilt
wots left of the ecosystem

in slopes
fake cattails
with real plants

evergreen and uniglory
in tugboat guise
margarett turebore

abreast the stoic ends
of manahatta, lashed
in bionic concrete

asphalt green
of the asphalt plant

ever further in the industrial landscape

reductio   this my hand
painterly the streetlight
w/ goldenrod
milf

the glory part of the hole
its apparent doom
rollerblading w/ huskies

adverse yaw
& colonoscopy fuel
readerly by starlight

I love emily like pasta
like indigestible globs of gluten

     as one hit—bleeding—
the racks—as it went apeshit therewithal
carnivalesque a smithy
near university x
coming home to a stump

ham is an 'exclusive' 'deal'
fresh outta scrunchies

dowisetripla
parabola
quidron estragon
18 cats next to me

pentimento cuz the painter repented
changed thir mind
'damp spleen'
is thir pet issue

chirping chicken
& hot yoga
solomon understood bird talk
with a magic ring

a soft coup
a wave of velvet revolutions
where albino fishes
swim with no eyes

not-so-great-scott
continued to lord it over everyone
and fetch it, perennial nigh
across 7 continents

penny a'left
person setting up accessories
in the gingkos
—a glove aloft—

blighted oaks
obelisk willo'whisp
4 abreast
xo from the distant past

lesser bandits
emerge from the obelisk
w/ sum hieroglyphic shit
then horus, strong-bull-appearing-in-thebes

bodily sun of the grotesques upglaring
strong-bull-beloved-of-ra
the noble youth
beloved like helen
when they shine on the horizon

to ra, like ra
like-ra-in-heaven
chosen-of-ra

grotesques w/ crab claws
upglaring from down
inna thicket
of manahatta its edge
whos to say wots
a good person anyway

pseudarchipelago

far from far abuts the sea

I wish I had more of your philosophy
that is to say the ssalt shall wend away
carrying along its axis certain
facts about the sea

lack of (it)
disallows my tong
frendeschip is a kindly orb
of whuch hole theories ben interpolat

nights I rede isidore
a moraliser w/ intimate knowledges
as far as east is from the west
one craves—third noon—

discoverd a name's
an elastic thing
one writes not so much about
as around homosexual desire

flesh and fell

and wen I am attird, thus arrayd
I sing of pretty things
to think that I 'suffer for nature'

who once disasspossessed
bankrolls the wind
rimmed by concrete
blastwalls and concertina wire
N CREEP INNA DARK
corner

tippling horns
cried that I was lordly
indecorously a moosehorn
atop a moose

I want to see you joust
on fixies
flawd tear ducts
& fake virginity

fingernail portrait
a sober business in york

heo unstressed becomes gallahad
call-ahead cousin
flibberty gibberty

horseshoe crab

lachrymose! a slouch of gilts
heady w/ hir pocket a'torn

n rested on its ledge
sno for thistleloo
if s/time it seems a bit out therr

betimes I am envious
                    —in grottoes

chavez calld it a photo finish
ı sucks honey ı eats nectar

hexametering the pythian
fraught w/ wireless fumes

I saw them all undulate
from where I pissed in the dunes

                    betimes I am envious
                        (in grottoes)

what the sno?!*%—
and its seersuck

there is sum fake
philanthropy to this city
some who sleep on what thir wing .
wd entirely cover up

day at the jersey shore

not guileless but aghast
a hawk in dove's coo
gay dogs in sultry summer
nudes and daytrippers ablaut
crab the fecund bay among
holly forest hermunculae
agape at the burning bank

what ys my anatomie

the glyph in ceremonye
or takes 1 (hermbug)

þt one is metamorphosd
inna fever (fervently) one's companions

from afar
glyph across tha distant globe

& how! (hallo) my circumstance
myn yt is
& non other

ffrosen seming herrabouts
surroundsound bilove
galyph in attitude (tha brine)

was choking
welwet amnesiac
in the hue & cry

hallow umbrage! and hallooo
transmagnified body!

—what ys hidden—
I will moan my song
on wham that yt ys on ylong

what is hidden in a circle
thirrby pronomounced odd

xe is my enemigma
& shall endure all my privlege

sconced hilt orr rod dilf
you may check me tomorrow

one may has
or may not
constabulize thir wytness

must thump
like a wave
to keep on cumming
to whuch ich have ben
disallowd y wake

agaynst the dobble bote
                    one es
alyve

the yellow tiles represent
a safety zone

one travelong to thir
erstwhal milieu

haggon paradimmatic
wan capitule as cd they
—none of it scared me rilly

cabs to and fro the burrito joint
el farolito   mija-hijo

friends sharing a headphone
when they goes under the bay

when the punchingbag was rocked
I made us all to huddle in the doorway

one's body will eat of
        the sutures

when one has no need
of a prosthesis

one ynvents a grammatical order
     (& haf done)

tromp loy ramshacklry
callin me everthing but the child of gawd

fiddleback
batterd but unbowd

up shit creek
w/o a shirpa

so to raise a stub aloft
to my computer made of meat

yr inner fish

safelier by shades
my brute companion

watching the deutsche bank
burn from the jersey shore

the sea was made
of lilleted sharks

avatar
           abattoir

30% chance of sno
who gets thir news from fishmongers

spun aground like a human candle
on the 4th of july

under the guise of cupid
thinking myself a very gay dog indeed

after a fashion antonioni

my flashiness, my coy
familiarity   that hopes
by flashing it
gets more familiar

my militant gay
longevity, millicent
making my throat
to go nascent

the suburbs
feel irreal
in your pocket
            an like t'engulf us

leisure permut
                    permutit

yardbirds
wrinkle the wall
spring feels like winter in this fever
                        —no   slower—
—against the beat—

spring was slow in coming
no harder luck than that forthcoming

banks of the ohio
on the dizzying banks themselves

cincinnati chili
in the park and seedy

angelic asthmatic
the mime mob gets us
to believe in the ball

the threads I were hit with
the train I were

licorice to rhyme
w/ icarus

dana says
how'd you get that cigarette
to look so famous?

fuck the fuck shit

for Darlington

talking of shakespeareian clam
& tadpole snax
they donned their merkins forsooth!
the pheasant hunt is hours away…

bedevilld homonym

bedevilld homonym dew...
                     : shagged your weird student
                            my lovers ashack
briny w/ plenary lemons
sporting shiny autos
                & went under
dorsey mcgonagall
                hefty then werr I
to apperciate new york (or newark was it)
whereas bart was a carpet, undulating w/ brine
         brink leffargy—ottomat

then (swete) my sweteing
         biblioteca lethargy (my moan amain)
homonym   (but brute)   advisory

herm of warsaw

piteous belief
party with a puff parade
herm of warsaw

flinging
emself in the rain
neuphilologische

feverfew—there—
tryst on the garden's bench
and they are all like *oh the hairy leg—*
get it in the moonlight!

windoun adown
hispano fr. in the vulgar register
erosion swung
oak withal

tennesseean you
are a pleasure
the junk e smokes withal

emself i' the fields
adamant the rain
follow alla people in orange

herm of warsaw
took es plans below
the sands of anbar
it's bye bye banyan time

o slow on the low

o slow on the low
to go amaying wit

w/ hawk-ears eaglet
    big-up   eagret

w/ pic and cor
I do what I like

who'd stop me
higher score in anime

po of authority enmixd
wit media entropy

        thots r all—stoppit
—over—n whut

beerdrinking claims
betterloving? clams're

not to be drunk and go
on loving.

they did, yo,
clam up a while.

a lost seagul eh wot
and some melting ice

en purgatoria del poesia

Yes I's drunk but I can build.
xxxx–kathryn l. pringle, *RIGHT NEW BIOLOGY*

god but these critters are cordial.
xxxx–Maureen Thorson, 'Swan Pitcher'

exposit the mulch   (həlp)
          @ wot point
          no longer — — — — -- war criimes
will ~~aye~~ or nil ~~aye~~
          n/t will come of n/t   (of
          finally fazed   woll exposit / war)
thir jellules   wot s/o urns
              to — — — cor — — — -- —
(revulsion)   in ikons
                  regrows thir hym
how! a thang — in berlioz (not ta use
conveniences err ————— not to be encased
in and/or <u>of</u> parts — — ta err flumox)
   (beggarly)
                    to s/o thir cheap muzick
(one culteur watches one gangsteur) (neither crazy nor)

up hill and down dale,
or get well thistleloo

–Liebchen, sweetness heart, what watch?
–Ten watch.
–Such much?
xxxx–*Casablanca*

why there is so adolescent-detective medium
veronic@
but th'angle displeases

but the amber is limerot, musculature
       a hunched aped retelling
       our president a dancing
       eight year nightmare
       the world was having

       the real surr
obliviating eel
being made to distinguish
having no real rigor
       since it must
(it will)
       the one
       white skate embargo

curliques on all speeds
       16, 78
the tighter the shorts
the harder they fall

person inna grey flannel suit
whatall you consent to walking down the street
hoboken wastrel
havelok kneeknockered
honeysuckle additioni

they're a fucking yakjob
fwd preaching

forced chivalry
nein underground
hollaback flasher-catchers
true confession magazines—
what thistleloo mislikes

maperson x

there cant be sheaves enuf aground
aflung the buttery steeps
something in my jamjar—
the number

having been given the number
balloons filled with blood
smattering furs
one's aggregate among lassoes

plying for some
agreed-upon consciousness, one hazards
a paradox of volcanic focus
a siblinghood

guarangine
kid of a preacherperson
you're ruining like, our whole day
whining for an exbox

liquid sunshine

for Dana Ward

as if waves are minions
the martens long crashing
you dont know what you—
till you—dont you
the desert is least desirous
of the sea
the parched basin is at least
ruptious or anxious craving
the sea and its grill of creatures

as if martens are minions
the waves're long crashing
the desert is least
and slantwise one must
be down w/ the crease
along the quaint crust
as if waves are minions
the martens long crashing

as if martens long crashing
the length of the river
the desert is at least like totally
whatever whatever whatever
at the pinnacle end of the sea
they want to put an ikea

I still dream but I know my dreams
are—dana, the
grill of birthstones
hiss in my teeth

swilling the myrtle I can't
get warm enough
black snow
I done got in
to that liquid sunshine

the tender martens
just aren't. my hair freezes
into dredcicles the lip
arched on a pin,

feeling dirty
was never any nohow
I hermorraged w/out thinking
a hundred dollars as I walked
down the street

place among the pawns
spawn of nil
nobody amid noperson
not even the word love

certain cheeses render me farcical
a grill in the half lite glinting
a quake on the brow the moment I came
half-awake to the prow to declare—
—here was the prow—
I mounted the dais
tardy and half-ill, but I stepped
to the podium I—mascara tear—
approached the platform I
opened my mouth
I began to declare—

a measure of perversion

My boo remains non-Googleable
xxxx—Jen Scappettone, *From Dame Quickly*

the sky was lousy with lightning
a plea for a measure of perversion
fairly grabbed one
who louche, lurking about
discoverd one's ordinary among fellawes

to triumvirate the workaday ~~icerink~~
       one was so impertinent as to produce a map
       without wearing a wig
       another was a wig emself

finally there were no more
gardens to repose in, and stories
was no longer louche in the french manner.

still they conducted themselves w/ resilient repose,
seeing how moribund a tack it were
to string stuff together like xmas necklaces
—but what wd emma do?

I never put much truck—on gesture—one reflects
on a declining lover most onerous
who signed the poison book and everything
where passionately one gazes
on the hops of VT
where grapes grow pommes among
and liberally the frown
dragonfly top dragonfly
n mumble their remains
teachers gossip, I've known worse
cases make beautiful deaths

washtub in the gowanus

We will continue to dismantle [-member?] Imagination with its pseudonym.
xxxx–Craig Watson

eat shit, hologram
sommavier re votre chambre
no clearance in niche
battling heavy sheaves

birds are netted
out of the sky
like fish

no trace herr of violence
but a slo meandering toward deth
bright peach conundrum
cleaves the ether

notes

All hs are aspirated.

elegy
ASTONISHED FISH:
'Why were the fish not given any tediousness,' from the poem
'Lost and Found' ('Achados e Perdidos') by Maria Esther Maciel,
in *O livro dos nomes* (The book of names).

gowanus
WHERE THE GOWANUS SPLITS IN TWAIN:
'rat light' —Alice Notley, *In the Pines.*

FIN CITY:
'IT'S 'FIN' CITY.' *NY Post* headline for an article about the
juvenile minke whale, nicknamed Sludgie, who died thrashing at
the mouth of the Gowanus Canal, 18 April 2007.

manahatta
MYTHS OF MANAHATTA:
'innumerable porpoises' qtd. in Evan Pritchard's *Native New Yorkers:
The Legacy of the Algonquin People of New York.*

pseudarchipelago
FLESH AND FELL:
'I want to see you joust on fixies.' —Christopher Warrington

WHAT YS MY ANATOMIE:
'Y wole mone my song / On wham þat hit ys on ylong.' –'When þe nyhtegale singes' MS Harley 2253 (early 14th cent.)

YR INNER FISH:
'Thinking myself a very gay dog indeed.' –Orson Welles, *The Lady from Shanghai*

A MEASURE OF PERVERSION:
'I've known worse cases make beautiful deaths.' –Evelyn Waugh, *Brideshead Revisited*

acknowledgments

Versions of these poems appear in *Shampoo Poetry 31, The Round Table, The Boog City Reader 2009, TRY!, EOAGH 5, Big Bridge 14: Slow Poetry, Boog City 64: Gay Pride Issue 2010, NO GENDER: Reflections on the Life & Work of kari edwards* (Litmus Press / Belladonna Books 2009), *Elective Affinities* and *Jacket 40*. Thank you to the editors. Several pieces appeared in a chapbook A *Buck in a Corridor* (flynpyntar 2008/2009).

Thanks to Ari Banias, Stefani Barber, Andrew Beccone, Rachel Bers, Brandon Brown, David Brazil, CAConrad, kari edwards, Dan Fisher, Paul Foster Johnson, Brenda Iijima, Rodney Koeneke, Kathleen Miller, Anna Moschovakis, Akilah Oliver, Tim Peterson (Trace), Cynthia Sailers, Inés Talamantez, Dana Ward, James Wagner, Alli Warren, Chris Warrington and Stephanie Young for their friendship, support and inspiration. Thanks especially to E. Tracy Grinnell.

colophon

The first edition of this book was published in 2011 in an edition of 1,000 copies, the first seventy-five of which were signed and numbered by the author and packaged with an accompanying letterpress broadside. This second printing was produced in 2019, and is limited to 500 copies.

Designed and typeset by goodutopian with text and titles set in Centaur and additional titles in Affair. Printed and bound by McNaughton & Gunn (Saline, Michigan). Mohawk Paper covers were printed offset at Prestige Printing (Brooklyn, New York) and foil stamped at Hodgins Engraving (Batavia, New York). Thanks to Serena Solin for design work on the second printing.

Ugly Duckling Presse (founded in 1993, and incorporated in 2003) is a nonprofit publisher for poetry, translation, experimental nonfiction, performance texts, and books by artists. Through the efforts of a volunteer editorial collective, UDP was transformed from a 1990s zine into a mission-driven small press that has published more than 300 titles to date, and produced countless prints and ephemera. A full catalog of our titles is available at www.uglyducklingpresse.org.

UDP is a 501(c)(3) nonprofit and registered charity in the State of New York, and a member of the Community of Literary Magazines and Presses (CLMP). We are grateful for the support of our individual donors and our subscribers. Please consider subscribing or making a tax-deductible donation.